CATHEI

CW01498334

A Life from Beginning to End

BY HOURLY HISTORY

Table of Contents

Introduction
Early Life at Court
A Young Widow
Taken Hostage
Henry's Last Wife
Becoming Queen
The Passing of a King
The Admiral's Wife
Catherine's Confessional
The Last Days of Catherine Parr
Conclusion
Bibliography

Introduction

Born in the summer of 1512 in England (the exact date and place is not known), Catherine Parr was the daughter of Sir Thomas Parr of Kendal and his wife Matilda "Maud" Green. Thomas Parr was a member of the nobility, descended from King Edward III, and ran in the same circle as Catherine's future husband, Henry VIII. Henry was a young man then and had just recently ascended to the throne as the king of England.

As a young child, Catherine often tugged along with her father during his service at the court. Little did she or anyone else realize the major role that she would play in the future. When Catherine's father perished abruptly in 1517 at the age of 39, Catherine's mother was left to raise her and her siblings on her own. Maud was an ambitious woman in her own right and served as a lady-in-waiting for King Henry's first wife, Catherine of Aragon. Here, she was able to shore up just the right kind of connections that would lead to a bright future for her children.

Maud lent her ambition to her daughter Catherine, who soon became actively involved in the court. Catherine also inherited her mother's keen intellect. She received an excellent education, becoming fluent in Latin, French, and Italian in addition to English, skills that were unusual for women of her time. Her mother ensured that Catherine and her siblings—William and Anne—knew the importance of learning and piety.

Nevertheless, Maud knew that it was the finding of a good marriage match that would be the most advantageous for Catherine's future. She began shopping around for a potential match when Catherine was just 11 years old. The first prospect was a young man by the name of Henry Scrope, who was the grandson of the affluent Thomas, Lord Dacre. However, this first proposal fell through, leaving Catherine to wait just a little while longer before she walked down the aisle. Before it was all said and done, she would walk down that fateful aisle more than once, and one day, one of those walks would have her arm in arm with one of England's most notorious kings.

Chapter One

Early Life at Court

"My hands are ordained to touch crowns and sceptres, not spindles and needles."

—Catherine Parr

After her first marriage proposal fell flat, Catherine waited a few more years before she once again considered her prospects. She was 16 and considered well-nigh ready for a husband when her mother Maud found a new eligible bachelor to be her suitor. She had arranged for her daughter to marry a 21-year-old gentleman by the name of Edward Borough.

Edward was the grandson of a much more troubled figure of the same name, the 2nd Baron Borough. The 2nd Baron Borough dealt with mental health issues throughout his life, which seemed to have cast a shadow on the whole Borough family. Nevertheless, Catherine was determined to make the best of the situation, and after marrying the younger Edward in 1529, she and her new husband made a life for themselves at his estate in Lincolnshire.

The Boroughs, despite their faults, were an affluent and notable family in the region. Even so, Lincolnshire was off the beaten path, and this fateful marriage would effectively exile Catherine from her life at the royal court over the next several years. Quite different from what she had been used to during her time in London, Lincolnshire had a very small circle of nobility. The Boroughs were one of the most affluent families in the region, but they were akin to being a small island in a sea of desolation.

Nevertheless, she counted her blessings. Catherine, at the very least, had a beautiful home where she could for the first time explore what it was like to be the lady of the house. Nestled in the heart of the town of Gainsborough, the Borough estate was the most impressive locale in the whole county. In fact, the manor still stands today and is a frequent tourist attraction. The home was constructed out of wood and red brick and came complete with a gatehouse and a moat. Inside the main house, there was a grand parlor, a drawing room, and extravagant and spacious chambers in which dances and other celebratory events were held. The west wing of the compound contained numerous bedrooms in which guests could sleep during their stay at the estate.

Despite this outward display of material wealth, the Borough family had a tragic shadow following it. As mentioned, Catherine's husband was the grandson of another Edward Borough, who struggled with mental illness for most of his life and had become a drain on family resources. He had perished in 1528, just prior to Catherine marrying his grandson, but the dark shadow of his life still hung heavily over the entire estate. So, too, did the debt that he had racked up.

It was the elder Borough's son (the father of the younger Edward Borough), Sir Thomas Borough, who did his best to pick up the pieces. While the family was certainly grateful for Thomas' efforts to steady the family ship, he was often demanding and draconian in the positions he took. After marrying into the Borough family, Catherine was expected to produce children to carry on the Borough name. Back in those days, producing a potential heir—especially a male heir—was considered of the utmost importance for the landed elites. She and her husband certainly tried to do so, but for whatever reason, they seemed destined to remain childless.

Catherine's mother Maud meanwhile perished in 1531. Interestingly enough, Maud was the same age as her late husband when he died; she was only 39 years old. It must have been hard on Catherine to lose her only remaining parent. She likely felt cut adrift without the guidance that she had so sorely depended on for much of her young life.

Just a couple of years later, she was in for another blow, for in 1533, her husband Edward abruptly passed away. Catherine, at just 20 years of age, was made a widow. She had no parents, no husband, and no children. Catherine was about as lonesome and isolated as could be. Her only safety net was that stern, former father-in-law of hers—Thomas. To his credit, Thomas took it upon himself to see to Catherine's needs, allotting her an allowance so that she could take care of herself. This was fairly generous, considering the fact that she had not yet given him any grandchildren. It was the first of many great kindnesses that Catherine Parr was shown during her life.

Chapter Two

A Young Widow

"Love maketh men like angels."

—Catherine Parr

After the death of her husband Edward Borough in 1533, Catherine Parr found herself holed up in Cumbria's Sizergh Castle. This was the ancestral home of the prominent Strickland family, and it's believed that Catherine spent a full 12 months here in mourning for her late first husband.

Catherine had close ties with the Stricklands. She was actually cousins with Catherine Neville—otherwise known as Lady Strickland—who oversaw the daily operations of the castle. Lady Strickland likely felt that it was her obligation to take care of her grieving cousin during her time of need. It was a time of grieving as well as a time of planning for the future. Catherine, after all, was still a young woman with her whole life ahead of her. Since, in those days, having a husband was of utmost importance for a woman in Catherine's position, it wasn't long before she began considering another matrimonial match.

This time, she wouldn't have the guiding light of her mother to lead her along, but fortunately, she did have the support of her cousin. It was Lady Strickland who helped to steer her in the direction of one of her distant relatives—John Neville, the 3rd Baron Latimer. Lord Latimer was nearly twice Catherine's age and had actually been married two times before. Both of his previous wives had perished, leaving him a widower.

Today, it might sound a bit suspicious for a man to have wives who perish one after the other—almost like the ingredients for a good mystery novel. But there was apparently nothing suspicious about the deaths of Lord Latimer's wives. Back in Catherine Parr's day, life was simply harder, and the mortality rate was much higher for everyone involved. Women also had to face much more difficult (and at times deadly) childbirths. This alone was enough to leave many men as widowers and in search of another wife.

Lord Latimer, as it were, very much needed a maternal figure for his motherless children, a fourteen-year-old boy and a nine-year-old girl. Catherine Parr was barely 22 years old at the time but was deemed to be a suitable enough stepmother for them both. It's said that sheer practicality for Catherine Parr and Lord Latimer was likely a big part of their relationship. Even so, Catherine would later look back rather fondly at the partnership.

The couple were married sometime in the summer of 1534. England was entering into a turbulent period at this point, with King Henry VIII at the helm. King Henry's problems, one could say, began with his first marriage. Henry married Catherine of Aragon, the widowed wife of his own brother, in June 1509. The marriage was initially a happy one, but after Catherine was seemingly unable to produce the son and heir to the throne that Henry craved, he sought to put his wife away.

Henry actually pointed to the fact that he had married the wife of his deceased brother as being a reason behind his misfortune. He brought up a biblical verse in Leviticus which casts aspersions on anyone who would marry his brother's wife. Context is of course everything when quibbling over Bible verses, but nevertheless, King Henry took this verse and ran with it. In fact, he ran all the way to Pope Clement VII, demanding an annulment of the marriage. The pope, however, didn't want to upset the Holy Roman Emperor Charles V, who just so happened to be Catherine of Aragon's nephew.

This caused a terrible standoff between the pope and the king of England, which was in its latter stages right around the time of Catherine Parr's marriage to Lord Latimer. Lord Latimer had, in fact, voiced his own opposition to King Henry VIII's desire to have his first wife put away and their marriage annulled. Nevertheless, King Henry, as stubborn as ever, was willing to do whatever it took to have his way. He ended up breaking with the pope and the Catholic Church completely and establishing himself as the head of the new Church of England just so he could unilaterally annul his marriage.

He finalized this effort in 1534 by enacting the so-called Act of Supremacy, which put him in charge of all theological affairs in England. This gave him the authority to—among other things—annul marriages. However, even before this act was passed by Parliament, Henry had secretly married a young lady of the court who had caught his eye, Anne Boleyn.

Lord Latimer and many others were repulsed by what had happened. How could the king toss aside the Catholic Church just so he could marry another woman? Over his own petty personal issues, Henry had set in motion tremendous forces that would alter the course of history in England forever. Catholics in Lincolnshire were infuriated by the breaking with the church, and in what was later called the Lincolnshire Rising, they rose up against the king and demanded that all good Catholics follow suit. They even came to Latimer and demanded he show his solidarity.

As mentioned, Latimer was just as repulsed as anyone else, but he wasn't about to mount an insurrection against the king. He may have quietly voiced his misgivings, but even so, he still felt compelled to publicly show support for the monarch. However, it was precisely his failure to join the anti-monarchy mob that resulted in him being seized by them and taken away.

While her husband was held hostage, Catherine Parr was left to her own machinations to take care of herself and her stepchildren. It seems that Catherine got along quite well with her stepdaughter but not so well with her stepson. It appears that these two rubbed each other the wrong way from the start—so much so that Catherine later reflected on the nature of the troubled relationship in some of her personal writings.

Nevertheless, with her husband gone, she found herself suddenly the head of her household. It's believed that it was during this difficult period of her life that Catherine Parr first formed a great dislike for Catholic fanatics and solidified her support for the Church of England, with King Henry at its head—a king who would someday soon become her husband.

Chapter Three

Taken Hostage

"I desire not to live, but to make it appear unto the world, that I live in Christ."

—Catherine Parr

From the fall of 1536 to the spring of 1537, Catherine Parr's life became a living nightmare. Turmoil had erupted after King Henry VIII decreed that the Church of England would officially split from the Catholic Church. Diehard Catholics who believed that the king was misguided and simply needed a certain amount of persuasion to change his mind were roaming the countryside, banding together in large mobs, ready to take action.

One of these mobs had already come to Catherine's door in Lincolnshire and basically kidnapped her husband. Lord Latimer was taken and forced into becoming a kind of spokesperson for the rebels. He was in a strange place since doing as much made him a traitor in the eyes of

King Henry, yet not giving in to the demands of those who had seized him likely would have meant certain death. Catherine Parr, in the meantime, was left alone as she sheltered at home with her two stepchildren.

In October 1536, this first uprising petered out, and the rebels agreed to surrender to the authorities. That December, a general amnesty was then issued. Latimer himself received notice that he needed to appear at the king's court in person to accept his clemency. As such, Latimer briefly returned to see his wife and children before heading off to London to plead his case. Bizarrely enough, the very fact that he was in London to denounce the rebellion and whatever perceived part anyone thought that he played in it was enough to provoke those same said disaffected rebels to seek vengeance against him and his family.

Lord Latimer, truly finding himself in a no-win situation, had become caught between the wrath of the king and the wrath of local rabble-rousers. And in January of 1537, when the next round of major revolt—the so-called Pilgrimage of Grace—gained momentum, his home was once again targeted.

The Pilgrimage of Grace was a popular uprising led by those same aforementioned

Catholics who wished to reverse King Henry's decision. There was also much more anger and resentment aimed at the king himself, for by this time, he had outraged public sentiment even further by executing his second wife, Anne Boleyn. Yes, after Anne failed to produce a male heir and otherwise provoked the ire of King Henry and his court, he had her arrested on some rather ludicrous charges of treason and adultery. She was executed in 1536.

So it was that this uprising by the Catholic faithful gained steam in January of 1537. The unruly mob made their way directly to Snape Castle while Lord Latimer was away pleading his case in London. They stormed into the place, stole whatever wasn't nailed down, and took Catherine and the children hostage. They then sent a messenger to deliver the news to Lord Latimer himself. He was bluntly informed that if he did not come to the castle directly, his family would be executed.

Even though the king's men were still in the process of threatening him with charges of treason, which could have him executed by the state, Latimer sped back to Snape Castle, where he confronted the mob. It's unclear exactly what happened next, but somehow, he managed to convince the rabble-rousers to let his family go.

The family had been severely traumatized, however, and unwilling to stay in the remote reaches of northern Lancashire any longer, they decided to move further south. They relocated to the Latimer property in Worcestershire before they moved on to Northamptonshire.

Not only was Catherine relieved to be in a more peaceful setting, but she was also happy to be closer to some of her surviving relatives. Among them were her beloved uncle, Sir William Parr of Horton, and his wife, Mary Salisbury, who lived at the Horton estate in Northamptonshire. After everything she had been through, Catherine Parr was desiring more than anything, just pure and simple peace. Little did she know, her new refuge would only be a brief respite.

Chapter Four

Henry's Last Wife

"Gentlemen, I desire company, but I have had more than enough of taking young wives, and I am now resolved to marry a widow."

—Henry VIII

Catherine Parr lived in the Northamptonshire estate from 1537 to 1542. During this time, she was often alone. Her husband Lord Latimer was a busy man who often headed back and forth from one place to another. Finally, in 1542, he would find his way to London, where he took part in several sessions of Parliament. Catherine, in the meantime, paid many visits to relatives who might support her husband and his cause. However, it was more or less a losing battle, as her husband's reputation was already ruined. Sadly, he perished a haunted and bitter man in February of 1543. He was buried at St. Paul's Cathedral that March.

His death once again placed Catherine Parr in free fall. She and her second husband had no children between them, and by all accounts, she was free to pursue her own interests. Even so, she still felt some responsibility to her stepchildren and was determined to see to it that they were well cared for in the aftermath of their father's demise. Aiding in this cause, Lord Latimer had left Catherine in charge of his estate in Northamptonshire, as well as additional funds to support his children.

Catherine had also become a mentor to another child entirely—a child of no small importance. That child was none other than Henry VIII's daughter Mary. Princess Mary was born from the ill-fated union between King Henry VIII and his first wife, Catherine of Aragon. Since her parents divorced, Mary had been quietly pushed to the side as her father continued his epic quest to produce a male heir to the throne. After having Anne Boleyn executed, he married Jane Seymour. Seymour would succeed in birthing a male child for the king—Edward—on October 12, 1537. It was a difficult birth, however, and she died soon afterward.

King Henry now had his son but was once again in search of a wife. He ended up marrying for a fourth time in 1540 to one Anne of Cleves. The marriage didn't work out very well, and Henry ended up getting it annulled that same year. He soon married again, this time to a 17-year-old girl named Catherine Howard. Sadly, Howard had a rough go of it, and in 1542, she ended up being charged with treason due to allegations that she had been unfaithful. She was found guilty as charged and executed.

It was this grisly opening that would lead King Henry VIII to turn his attention toward Catherine Parr in 1543. Catherine's husband had just perished, and as mentioned, Catherine had been cultivating a relationship with Henry's neglected daughter from his first marriage—Mary. Yes, the future Bloody Mary herself was in need of a motherly mentor, and Catherine Parr was proving ready to fill that role, even before she caught the eye of the incessantly bride-seeking King Henry.

One of the first major cues of the king's interest came when Catherine's brother William was suddenly made chief steward and receiver of Writtle. This was a coveted post, and the fact that the king was willing to grant it to William indicated that he expected a favor in return. Catherine herself is said to have remarked that her brother was likely the happiest person among them in light of her marriage prospects to the king. Nevertheless, the two were ultimately wed on July 12, 1543.

This latest and last wedding of King Henry VIII was a rather sedate affair, held in front of a modest gathering of friends and family. Among these family and friends were those who were somehow connected to the king's former ill-fated wives. Although no one dared condemn the king for his previous actions, their somber stares must have had an effect on Catherine Parr as she walked down the aisle. Still, the 30-year-old Catherine Parr stood prim and proper in her wedding dress, with her long red hair flowing down over her thin frame.

The trim form of Catherine stood in stark contrast with the gargantuan and imposing figure of the king. In his youth, King Henry was said to have been an attractive, fit, and athletic prince. He was now 52 and morbidly obese, with a ruddy, agitated expression permanently fixed on his face. Still, most women of the day couldn't help but be thrilled at the prospect of marrying a king and becoming a queen. And if Catherine Parr did have any real misgivings about her latest matrimonial match, she most certainly kept those feelings to herself.

Chapter Five

Becoming Queen

"Being appointed Regent of this realm in the king's absence, and understanding from Shrewsbury your diligent service done in the office committed to you, both for defense of the borders and chastising of the king's enemies, we give you hearty thanks and require you to give the like in our name to the captains and gentlemen who have served you."

—Catherine Parr

Despite any potential misgivings, Catherine Parr settled into her role as queen quite well. She seemed to genuinely enjoy the role and set about doing her duties to the fullest. She also found herself in a great position to enact some of her own beliefs since King Henry was at the center of the storm of religious reform that had been unleashed by the annulment of his first marriage.

Those who were in favor of reform and agreed with the break with the Catholic Church quietly encouraged Catherine to pursue the marriage as a means of furthering their agenda. Catherine herself had by this point come out fully in favor of religious reform. Her decision to come out as a reformer was in no small part due to her rough treatment at the hands of hardline Catholic radicals years earlier. Catherine and her supporters felt that she would be in the best position possible as queen to help direct the undercurrents of reform that were still rippling through the kingdom after King Henry's decision to break with the Catholic Church.

As mentioned, Catherine also positioned herself as a supporter of the once-spurned Princess Mary. Contrary to Henry's previous wives, Catherine got on quite famously with Mary, and her alliance with her would have tremendous implications for the future of England. Catherine set about reconciling Princess Mary with the king, restoring her as a potential heir to the throne.

Catherine also had keen eyes for the international scene. She realized that England was in a much more precarious place now that King Henry had cut ties with the Catholic Church. His first wife that he had put away— Catherine of Aragorn—was the aunt of Emperor Charles V. Charles was in charge of the massive conglomeration of Western and Central European states known then as the Holy Roman Empire. It was his influence that had caused the pope to dither as it pertained to King Henry's requested annulment. The pope didn't dare spark the wrath of Charles V by pulling the rug out from under his aunt, Catherine of Aragon. Nevertheless, Henry did what he wanted regardless; Catherine was put away, and a rift was created between England and the powerful emperor.

Just as she tried to ease the rift between King Henry and his daughter Mary, Catherine Parr tried to reduce the tension between Henry and Charles. Catherine herself was a bit conflicted, however, since she seemed to be playing both sides of the fence. She seemed to want to patch up relations with the Holy Roman Empire while also embracing the reformers unleashed by her husband, the king. She also supported Princess Mary, who had already made clear that she supported the Catholic Church over the reformers.

It's been said that Catherine hoped that Mary, should she ever rise to the throne, would be able to balance her own beliefs with those of the reformers. This, of course, is most certainly not how history played out since the future

Queen Mary would usher in much bloodshed (hence her nickname Bloody Mary) as she attempted to turn back the clock and restore Catholicism to England.

It's important to note that along with cultivating her relationship with her stepdaughter Mary, Catherine also became close to her other stepdaughter, Elizabeth. Elizabeth was the daughter of the ill-fated union between King Henry and his second wife, Anne Boleyn. No one knew, at this point, that little Elizabeth would eventually rise up to the position of queen, but her stepmother Catherine Parr would have a lasting influence on her both as it pertained to her religious views and her perspectives on romance and marriage.

Catherine, of course, was eager to forge relations with the crown prince as well. She was keen to see to it that young Prince Edward might throw in his lot with the reformers. By 1544, when Edward was only six years old, King Henry was already establishing a princely household for him, complete with his own tutors and advisers. Catherine was involved in the appointment of some of these tutors, most notably in the selection of Richard Cox and John Cheke, the latter of which was a most dedicated reformer. Also in Catherine's inner circle were her former stepdaughter Margaret Neville, her cousin Maud, her uncle Lord William Parr of Horton, and even her former stepson John's wife, a woman by the name of Lucy Somerset. This core group would be of great importance when King Henry left England in order to lead the English troops in France.

Relations with the French had by this point soured. The French had irritated King Henry by aiding rebels up in Scotland, and for him, this was enough to merit intervention. Henry had declared war on the French and was now staging an invasion of the French stronghold of Boulogne. In his absence, Henry put his new wife Catherine Parr in place as regent. This, of course, demonstrated the high level of trust that King Henry VIII had in his queen.

Utilizing the strengths of her inner circle, Catherine was quite effective during her tenure in the executive role. While she reigned in Henry's stead, she managed the royal treasury, ensured the smooth administration of justice, and maintained order. She also corresponded with foreign dignitaries and handled diplomatic affairs. Catherine was clearly intelligent and proved herself more than capable of handling the responsibilities of queenship. Her two stepdaughters, Mary and Elizabeth, bore witness to all of this, and it seems that they were highly influenced by the way Catherine took charge.

The most direct influence Catherine Parr had, however, was the fact that she convinced her husband to put his two daughters back into the line of succession. Prior to Catherine coming onto the scene, both girls had been declared illegitimate after Henry had put their mothers away. In the tumultuous years ahead, Catherine Parr—the lone soul who seemed to show these troubled children any real concern and affection at all—would remain an inspiration to them both.

Boulogne, in the meantime, fell to the English on September 14, 1544. King Henry VIII ordered his troops to restrain themselves and allow the civilian population to evacuate with their goods unmolested. It's said that Henry's troops followed his orders in part, allowing the refugees to travel several miles out of the king's sight without suffering any duress. It was only when they were beyond the sight of the king that the more bloodthirsty English soldiers began to plunder the refugee train in clear defiance of Henry's orders. These troops had been promised plunder by their captains, and regardless of what the king had told them, they were determined to get it.

After this evacuation of the locals, King Henry entered Boulogne to bask in his glory and triumph. His victory, however, would be undermined when he learned that on the very same day that he had conquered Boulogne, Charles V of the Holy Roman Empire had signed his own separate peace treaty with France. Ultimately, King Francis of France was forced to sign a treaty that gave Henry the rights to Boulogne for eight years, after which the king of France would be allowed to pay a heavy sum of money to get it back.

At any rate, Catherine Parr's success as queen and regent would be even more consequential than this one lone battlefield victory.

Chapter Six

The Passing of a King

Many thanks for the letter that you last sent me, dearest mother; which is a token of your singular and daily love for me. And now, as it hath seemed good to God; the greatest and best of beings, that my father and your husband, our most illustrious sovereign, should end this life, it is a common grief to both. This, however, consoles us, that he is now in heaven, and that he hath gone out of this miserable world into happy and everlasting blessedness."

—Edward VI

King Henry VIII returned from his military campaign in France in October of 1544. He was ready to bask in his triumph, but his own health was fading fast. Henry was morbidly obese and suffering from a wide variety of ailments, such as gout, leg ulcers, and excruciating headaches. In light of Henry's many difficulties, his wife and queen, Catherine Parr, not only took on more duties at court but also served as the primary parent for Henry's children.

Her statecraft, in fact, was increasingly more attractive than King Henry's, and by 1545, it seemed that much of the international scene had turned against England. One means of offsetting this imbalance would have been for England to align itself with the growing Protestant faction in Europe. It's unclear whether or not Queen Catherine encouraged such a move, but her later successor, Elizabeth, most certainly would.

During this period, Catherine also wrote several books. In 1544, she published her *Psalms or Prayers Taken Out of Holy Scriptures*, to be followed in 1545 by *Prayers or Meditations*. Both books were bestsellers at the time. Some of her written commentaries, however, would provoke suspicion from conservative officials who questioned what the queen's religious allegiance really was. The bishop of Winchester and a certain Lord Wriothesley even sought to bring charges of heresy against her.

According to the famous *Foxe's Book of Martyrs*, they very nearly succeeded because, even more dangerously, Catherine often engaged her husband in debates on religious matters— debates which she often won. This dynamic began to irritate Henry, who complained to his ministers, "A good hearing it is when women become such clerks; and a thing much to my comfort, to come in mine old days to be taught by my wife."

Charges were then drawn up against Catherine Parr, but fortunately, she learned of the plot just in time. When Henry attempted to entrap her in a religious dispute, Catherine skillfully navigated the situation. She said that she merely discussed religion with him to help "pass away the pain and weariness of your present infirmity" and that she simply hoped to profit from "your Majesty's learned discourse." This last-minute submission apparently appeased Henry, and the matter was promptly dropped. Catherine was, of course, relieved by the outcome. She would keep her head down and not publish any more books until after her husband's death. Others who died on both sides of the divide—Protestant and Catholic—would not be quite so lucky.

By the spring of 1546, the king's health was in serious decline. It's recorded that he had some sort of medical episode during this period, which briefly rendered him bedridden. Catherine, who had played the part of the king's unofficial nurse since the start of their marriage, was closely attending him during his initial round of sickness. The king once again fell ill that December and became progressively worse from there on out. Historians believe that the last time Catherine saw Henry was on Christmas Eve. For whatever reason, after this point, he was kept quietly away from the queen.

Catherine was in a personal quandary of a whole other sort as well. Just prior to her marriage to the king, she had become acquainted with a gentleman by the name of Thomas Seymour. Seymour was a dashing admiral with whom Catherine had become quite smitten just as King Henry came calling. He was also the brother of Jane Seymour, the former wife of King Henry. This made him Crown Prince Edward's uncle, which gave him substantial clout in the royal court. From the very start, Catherine Parr truly enjoyed Thomas Seymour's company. He was charming, handsome, and very ambitious. As mentioned, though, Catherine by no means felt she could deny King Henry's advances. With the king now in failing health, however, in her heart of hearts, she likely couldn't help but wonder if the flame once lit with Thomas Seymour might yet be rekindled.

At any rate, the intervening weeks are said to have been of high anxiety for Catherine Parr. Not only was she worried about her husband, but she was also worried about what might become of her after he passed. On January 27, 1547, Henry was informed by his doctors that his case was hopeless. He was told that he was not likely to live much longer. It was then on the very next day that King Henry VIII finally succumbed to his many ailments.

Chapter Seven

The Admiral's Wife

"I would not have you think that this mine honest goodwill towards you to proceed of any sudden motion of passion; for, as truly as God is God, my mind was fully bent, the other time I was at liberty, to marry you before any man I know."

—Catherine Parr

Decked out in a stunning blue velvet dress and sporting a so-called widow's ring for the occasion, Catherine solemnly stood watch as King Henry VIII was put to rest. Interestingly, even though he had broken with the Catholic Church during his life, Henry had firmly stipulated that he be given the standard, traditional Latin rites after his death. Demonstrating just how complicated England's break with the Roman Catholic Church was, the very man who initiated the break still craved a good old-fashioned Catholic wake.

Henry was interred next to his former wife Jane Seymour on February 16, 1547. Jane was the mother of the heir to the throne—Crown Prince Edward. She had perished during childbirth and subsequently hadn't had the chance to get on the king's bad side. Her final resting place, therefore, was already secure.

Catherine Parr, Henry's last and final wife, was still very much alive and looking toward what the future might bring. She was now considered a dowager queen, and her attentions would be firmly focused on the transition of kingship from her late husband to that of the crown prince. The crown passed directly to Henry's male heir, even though his revised will allowed for power to also pass to Mary and then Elizabeth if something were to happen to Edward.

Along with the royal line of succession, Catherine Parr also had to consider her own well-being. Each time she had lost a husband, it had brought forth its own unique period of instability. Fortunately for her, King Henry had made sure that she would be well taken care of after his passing. She was given a generous allowance, and Henry had stated that she should still be given the respect of a queen, even after he was dead. Nevertheless, King Henry, mindful of some of the controversy she had stirred up with her religious views, was sure to clip her wings of power. While she would be a well-cared-for queen dowager, she would have no executive power in the aftermath of her husband's demise.

With the passing of the king, it wasn't long before Catherine Parr turned her attention back to her old paramour, Thomas Seymour. However, Seymour was himself preoccupied. As a high-ranking nobleman of the court, he was seeking to marry up, but not by way of marrying a former queen. He was actually seeking the hand of one of the deceased king's daughters, Mary or Elizabeth. According to surviving correspondence, it seems that he had the keenest interest in young Elizabeth, who was 13 at the time.

Considering the fact that Elizabeth was now third in line to the throne, it doesn't seem that Thomas was hoping to become king—he was merely seeking the financial and social windfall of marrying into the royal family. At any rate, Thomas Seymour, who was nearly 40 at the time, fired off an official proposal by written letter directly to Elizabeth. Elizabeth was apparently quite shocked to receive it and expressed as much in her response.

She carefully stated that while she was certainly flattered, she wasn't yet ready for marriage. She cited both her young age and her mental state. She also mentioned the death of her father and her state of mourning as part of her rationale for not being ready to go down the aisle. Elizabeth wrote that she needed at least two years to consider his offer. She ended the letter by artfully remarking on how she simply felt that there was no choice but for her to reject Thomas Seymour's offer of marital bliss. She then stated that, at the very least, she hoped that she could remain Seymour's "good friend."

It was indeed a rather longwinded and diplomatic way for this young girl to suggest to the older gentleman that they simply be friends and eschew any notion (at least for the foreseeable future) of holy matrimony. Considering Elizabeth's closeness to her stepmother Catherine, one can only wonder if Catherine's own hand might have guided this youngster in the words she chose in her carefully crafted rejection of Thomas Seymour's proposal. Catherine had actually been made the then 13-year-old Elizabeth's guardian at the time, so the closeness of their proximity makes such a thing seem perhaps even likely.

Even though she was the guardian of one of the princesses, Catherine no longer stayed at court. Instead, she packed up her things and took Elizabeth with her to a new household in Chelsea, where they set up shop sometime in the middle of March 1547. Catherine had indeed been well taken care of financially. She had been given cash and valuable property, and it was at the Chelsea Manor, located just west of London, that Catherine and Elizabeth settled into their new lives.

Catherine was now 35 years old. She was older and wiser but was still young enough to try to start anew. And it wasn't long before the aforementioned Thomas Seymour became a part of her plans. Although not a whole lot is known about the quiet courtship that began to evolve, it is believed that he became a frequent visitor at the Chelsea Manor. Scholars also tend to agree that it must have been sometime in the month of May in that same fateful year of 1547 that this couple decided to get married.

Even so, the couple kept their relationship as quiet as possible to avoid critics who would undoubtedly express they were not waiting long enough after the king's demise. There was also the worry that if Catherine conceived a child with Thomas so soon after Henry's death, there could be confusion about the child's paternity. Such confusion would not only have been inconvenient but very troubling for the entire kingdom.

Nevertheless, the couple got married by the end of May. They did so in secret and initially led everyone to believe that they were simply engaged. This, in itself, generated friction in court since many were put off by the very notion of their relationship. Even worse for Catherine was the anger provoked in Princess Mary, who was outraged that her stepmother would want to marry so soon after her father's death. Thomas himself approached Mary to see if she could soothe things over with the king's council, but she flat-out refused. She also loudly voiced her displeasure with her half-sister Elizabeth, which the queen dowager found to be very troubling indeed. Catherine Parr, after all, had tried her best to soothe and mend the damaged relations between Mary and her father. Yet now, she had managed to rupture her own relationship with a young woman to whom she had previously been close.

Unable to persuade Mary, Thomas and Catherine decided to address King Edward VI directly. They did so by approaching one of the king's confidantes, John Fowler. Thomas and

Catherine asked Fowler to inquire with the king for them to see that he might give his blessing to their marriage. It's important to remember that Thomas and Catherine were already secretly married at this point. They were essentially pretending not to be married and were actually seeking a marital blessing after the fact. Finally, Thomas managed to get a private audience with his nephew, the young King Edward. Edward, fond of his stepmother Catherine, eventually gave his approval.

At last, the couple got the blessing that they craved. Yet the damage was already done. Princess Mary, in particular, was outraged at what she took to be a complete show of disrespect to her father's memory. Catherine heard more than a few snide remarks when she went to court, and on one occasion, an irate duchess even got into a shoving match with her. Yes, while the lives of the modern-day royal family might seem dramatic, it was just as bad or worse back in the days of Catherine Parr.

Despite the insults, Catherine insisted that until King Edward VI married a queen of his own, she deserved respect as the queen dowager. According to Henry's last will and testament, her claims were backed up on legal grounds. Nevertheless, there were many in the court who were more than willing to disregard it. Catherine, as strong of a front as she put on, was only human, and the slights ultimately became a bit too much for her to bear. In her frustration, she soon began to have second thoughts about her marriage—a marriage which had her downgrade herself from being the queen dowager to the wife of an admiral.

Chapter Eight

Catherine's Confessional

"Behold, Lord, how I come to You: a sinner, sick and grievously wounded. I am not asking for bread, but for the crumbs that fall from the children's table. Cast me not out of Your presence, although I deserve to be cast into hell fire. If I should look upon my sins, and not upon Your mercy, I should despair. For in myself I find nothing to save me, but a dunghill of wickedness to condemn me."

—Catherine Parr

By the late summer of 1547, Catherine Parr and her new husband had found themselves royal outcasts. Not only that but they were being shunted so vigorously to the side that they seemingly had to fight for every morsel of possible recognition they felt was owed them.

This was most painfully made clear when Catherine's jewels were denied her. These were stored in the Tower of London, and Catherine fully expected their return. Yet, upon asking for them, she was told that they no longer belonged to her. This was preposterous to Catherine since some of the items, including an expensive gold cross that was given to her by her mother, predated her marriage to King Henry VIII. She and Thomas filed a legal complaint over the matter. But it ended up being a losing battle, and Catherine would perish before ever seeing any of those beloved artifacts that had been stashed in the Tower.

Catherine, in her last days, would become increasingly bitter over her situation and ultimately chose to withdraw to her Chelsea Manor. Here, she could live like a queen, even if the rest of the court didn't acknowledge her as such. In fact, it's said that after her own inner circle flocked to the Chelsea Manor, she basically created a secondary court all of her own.

It was while Catherine was forging this personal refuge that the chaos accompanying England's religious reformation began to escalate further. While King Henry VIII had started the process with his break from the

Catholic Church, Henry didn't disagree so much with Catholic doctrine as he simply disagreed with the authority of the pope. Taking the powers of the pope onto his own person, Henry had made himself the head of his own Church of England. This opened the door for subsequent Protestant reformers to demand not only that England turn away from the authority of the pope but also dismiss many other aspects of Catholic dogma.

Young King Edward VI was now at the center of this storm, and his Protestant advisors repeatedly pressed him to enact legislation supporting reform. As was the case in 1547, when he was convinced to pass the so-called Election of Bishops Act. This bit of legislation likely seemed like a pragmatic evolution of King Henry's prerogative since it called for giving the king the authority to appoint his own bishops and archbishops.

The following spring, a much more organic yet altogether significant change occurred when most of the churches in London began to conduct services in English. In the past, Catholic churches insisted on carrying out rites in the Latin language. Now, they were spoken in English so that all the parishioners could hear and readily understand what was being said. It was around this time that Archbishop Cranmer achieved another milestone by issuing the first *Book of Common Prayer* for the consumption of the masses.

Catherine herself was a champion of all these reforms and made sure to make her home in Chelsea Manor reflective of the prevailing Protestant spirit of the time. She even went so far as to publish another book on the subject, a personal testament on her own experience with the Protestant faith entitled *The Lamentation of a Sinner*. Even though this is considered a Protestant work, it very easily could have taken its cues from Catholic theologian St. Augustine's classic work *Confessions*. In a similar manner, Catherine outlines her previous faults as a sinner and how she has learned to seek redemption through God's grace.

The book spoke of enduring hardships and difficulties, and Catherine Parr would certainly have plenty of those ahead of her.

Chapter Nine

The Last Days of Catherine Parr

"Now, I often mourn and complain of the miseries of this life, and with sorrow and great heaviness suffer them. For many things happen daily to me which oftentimes trouble me, making me heavy, and darken mine understanding."

—Catherine Parr

If it wasn't bad enough that Catherine had become spurned by high society in London's royal court, by 1548, she began to have problems in her own home. The problems arose from an area that caught Catherine by complete surprise, although in many ways it should have been predictable.

Catherine was still Elizabeth's guardian, and after she married Thomas Seymour, he too had become a kind of guardian. In essence, he was Elizabeth's stepfather. This created a rather awkward situation since Thomas had previously proposed to the young girl. Elizabeth was 14 years old by this point, and although today such an age is considered incredibly young, back then it was a typical age for marriage.

Even though Thomas had been spurned by Elizabeth in the past, he still couldn't resist flirting with her. Some of this was apparently done right under Catherine's nose, and initially, she thought it was just innocent, good fun. Catherine, for example, was fond of holding dances, and it wasn't long before Thomas began to ask Elizabeth to be his dance partner. Elizabeth typically presented herself to Thomas in a shy, coy manner, and the whole encounter was usually a cause of laughter for all.

But underneath the laughter, Thomas was quietly eyeing Elizabeth as if sizing her up. Thomas thought that despite her previous rejection, Elizabeth actually did seem to have some feelings for him. It was after he came to this conclusion that Thomas began to press his luck. While staying at Chelsea Manor, there were mornings he would step right into Elizabeth's room to say hello when she was still in bed. Such things were entirely against protocol. Even if it were just an innocent greeting, the mere action of entering the young girl's room was considered bad form. Thomas then proceeded to create a scene on another occasion when he actually leaned over her bed to kiss her, which prompted an attendant to chase him from the room.

Catherine seems to have been a bit deluded by what was happening around her. For a time, she insisted that her husband was just having good fun or showing his affection. There were times that she, too, joined in on this supposed fun, under the belief that it was indeed just innocent playfulness. There was an incident, for example, in which Catherine, Elizabeth, and Thomas lay in bed together as a hysterical Elizabeth was tickled by them both. For Catherine, they were just playing and joking like joyful children. But surely, some small part of her must have realized something was off. She seemed to be trying to normalize her husband's predations, and by doing so, she only made him bolder in his actions.

Catherine, however, was about to become distracted in a big way. In February of 1548, she came to realize that she was pregnant. Throughout all her previous marriages, she had never conceived. In many ways, she had likely given up on such things, yet now at age 35, she was about to bear fruit. It was a joyous occasion for both Catherine and Thomas, who were excited at the prospect of their union bringing forth a human life. Even so, Catherine couldn't help but have some trepidation.

Having children at an older age tends to bring more complications, and back in the sixteenth century, these complications could quite easily lead to death. Increasing her doubts was the fact that from the beginning of her pregnancy, she felt quite ill, and the severity of her ailments was hard to dismiss. Perhaps exacerbating her troubles was an increasing concern about Thomas and Elizabeth's relationship. It seems that it was after she became pregnant and began to slow down and pay closer attention to what was happening around her that her suspicions finally began to rise.

Things then came to a sudden and alarming head when Catherine made her way into Elizabeth's bedroom on a May morning in 1548, only to find Thomas and Elizabeth locked in a loving embrace. No longer finding the antics playful or amusing, Catherine condemned them both for the display of intimacy. She was upset with what felt like a terrible betrayal. She was also haunted by the deeper, even more complex emotions of fear and guilt. She felt guilty that she had failed Elizabeth as her guardian. At the same time, she was also struck with fear because she knew that if these happenings got out, it would cause a terrible scandal.

Her tortured brain struggled desperately to find a solution to her dilemma. Catherine, with a heavy heart, realized that the best thing she could do was have Elizabeth move out of the house. Today, it might seem outrageous that a minor would be kicked out of the house because of the predation of their stepfather. But in Catherine's world, in which reputation was everything, the safeguarding of what little reputation that she and Thomas had left took precedence over everything else. And if she felt that quietly moving her stepdaughter to another location would prevent the spread of gossip, she was willing to do that.

She inquired with a couple of nearby friends—Sir Anthony and Lady Denny—and asked if they might allow Elizabeth to lodge with them for a time. They agreed, thereby giving Catherine a means of separating her stepdaughter from Thomas. Before running the child off, Catherine had one final heart-to-heart with her. During this exchange, Catherine apparently gave Elizabeth one last piece of advice; she advised her to protect her reputation at all costs. This was indeed something that Elizabeth, who never married as queen, seemed to take to heart.

For what it was worth, this parting was the very last time that Catherine and Elizabeth would see each other, for Catherine herself was not long for this world.

Conclusion

Catherine's pregnancy was a difficult one, and the summer of 1548 did not make things easier for her. It was extremely hot that year, and by late July, terrible, drought-like conditions were prominent. Even worse, there was also an outbreak of plague. Catherine often felt sick in the heat, and fears of contamination from the outbreak of plague haunted her every moment.

Although the cause of disease was not well known in those days, it was readily understood that population centers carried the outbreak. As such, Catherine thought it prudent to distance herself as far from London as possible. They ended up in Sudeley Castle, nestled in Gloucestershire. Here, Catherine and Thomas had everything they needed, including specially prepared rooms full of attendants for the moment that Catherine would give birth.

Catherine spent these days in quiet reflection. During these moments, she began to harbor increasing resentment toward Thomas for his role in what had happened with Elizabeth. At the same time, Catherine was in frequent correspondence with not only Elizabeth but also Princess Mary. The two had just embarked upon a kind of rapprochement. Shortly thereafter, on August 30, 1548, Catherine's long-awaited child—a daughter named Mary—was born. Sadly, Catherine was not well, and her health continued to worsen. Just a few days later, on September 5, she passed away from what was "childbed fever."

Catherine Parr died, leaving a troubled world in her wake—a world in which Protestant fought Catholic, and Catholic fought Protestant. The stability of England rested on the shoulders of the boy King Edward VI, who would perish just a few years after his stepmother. The struggle for both power and religious conviction would then continue with Mary and Elizabeth. Difficult times were ahead.

Bibliography

Foxe, John (1563). *Foxe's Book of Martyrs*.

McDowall, David (1989). *An Illustrated History of Britain*.

Norton, Elizabeth (2010). *Catherine Parr: Wife, Widow, Mother, Survivor, the Story of the Last Queen of Henry VIII*.

Porter, Linda (2010). *Katherine the Queen: The Remarkable life of Katherine Parr, the Last Wife of Henry VIII*.

Susan, James (1999). *Kateryn Parr: The Making of a Queen*.

Susan, James (2008). *Catherine Parr: Henry VIII's Last Love*.

Weir, Alison (2007). *The Six Wives of Henry VIII: Find out the truth about Henry VIII's wives*.

The Tudor Society.
https://www.tudorsociety.com/

Historic Royal Palaces.
https://www.hrp.org.uk/

Printed in Dunstable, United Kingdom